by Nancy Van Laan

IN A CIRCLE LONG AGO

A TREASURY OF NATIVE LORE FROM NORTH AMERICA

illustrated by Lisa Desimini

SCHOLASTIC INC.

New York   Toronto   London   Auckland   Sydney

This book is dedicated to the legend keepers of
the past and to those who still tell them.

—N. V. L.

For my family and friends

—L. D.

The artist has chosen several different techniques and styles in creating the
illustrations for this book, including acrylics, found objects, collage, oil
paints, and watercolors, in order to reflect the unique mood of each tale.

ISBN 0-590-16383-3

Text copyright © 1995 by Nancy Van Laan.
Illustrations copyright © 1995 by Lisa Desimini
All rights reserved.
Published by Scholastic Inc., 555 Broadway, New York, NY 10012,
by arrangement with Alfred A. Knopf, Inc.

12 11 10 9 8 7 6 5 4 3 2 1   6 7 8 9/9 0 1/0

Printed in the U.S.A.   09

First Scholastic printing, November 1996

CONTENTS

INTRODUCTION

As a child, I spent several years living on my grandfather's ranch in Southern California. His adobe home was situated on top of a wide mesa, near a Cahuilla burial ground, and we were always finding relics in the deep canyon just beyond. Most evenings, my grandfather would sit us down and show off his collection of arrowheads, pottery fragments, and other artifacts. He told us legends and stories, particularly ones that originated in California and the Southwest. And he taught us to respect those who lived across this vast continent long before white people came.

In addition, my father constantly pointed out to his children anything he felt was important to know about nature. We learned about birds, animals, rocks, oceans, the stars and everything else in the sky, even the weather. Early on, he instilled in us a strong appreciation of our natural environment.

It was through my grandfather's and my father's consistent teaching that I gained an understanding of the world as the native peoples of this land always knew it to be. In turn, this knowledge made me aware of the loss of many unique cultures because of the intrusion of white people—my people.

Around ten years ago, these memories came back to haunt me. One warm Sunday in May, while driving down a country road in Bucks County, Pennsylvania, I passed the Churchville Nature Center. Noticing a small crowd, I decided to see what was going on. In a field, the Lenape were performing their annual traditional corn-planting ceremony. I watched as the tribal elder chanted prayers; then the women danced before planting corn in four parts of a circle. Later, when the elder stood in the circle to tell legends, it dawned on me why I might have chosen to wander down this particular road—a part of me said it was time to rekindle some of those lost feelings I'd had. Somehow I was going to have to come to terms with the whiteness of my own skin. Maybe doing so would allow my roots to intertwine with the native peoples' of this land, at least in spirit.

I listened closely as Bill Whip-poor-will Thompson explained how fire and maple syrup came to be, and related so many other wonderful tales, beautifully told. Then, because I write for children, I thought of somehow getting the stories into print for young readers, to help them learn what had been taught to me as a child— deep respect for those who first lived in this land.

Eventually, I asked Bill for permission to publish a legend called "Rainbow Crow." His immediate enthusiasm was reassuring. He couldn't write, or so he said, and he worried about what would happen to the legend after he was no longer around to tell it.

As a result of the publication of that book, storytellers from other regions encouraged me to do more. Soon, I knew I wanted an anthology of legends to be my next project. I realized, though, that before I could actually sit down and adapt them, I had to understand each one's intent, the way the keeper of the legend does. It was then that it became clear how little I knew and how much I needed to learn.

Just over four hundred years ago in North America, there were more than three hundred languages as different as Norwegian is from English, spoken by as many tribes of native people. Some are still heard on reservations today. Likewise, tribes, or individual bands within a tribe, still get together, hold dances and ceremonies, and share the rich culture of their past.

These ceremonies or legends are often unique to a single band within a tribe. For example, there are traditions practiced by the Blackfeet in Alberta that are different from traditions of the Blackfeet living on reservations in Montana. On the other hand, one tale will often be very like another from a completely different culture, such as stories about Fox told in the Far North that are like Coyote tales from the Southwest. Quite a few told in the Southeast are similar to stories found in Africa or Asia. How did this happen? Nobody is really sure, but I would like to think that if somewhere in the past, one of these native peoples knew that this was so, a legend would have been told to explain why.

Many tribes believe their legends should be told only during the long months of winter. The Ojibwa and the Omaha say that legends related during the warm months will encourage snakes to multiply. And certain Plains tribes indicate that Coyote tales should be told only when snakes are visible. Different tribes hold different beliefs about all things, including the best time to tell a story.

The path chosen for this collection forms a spiral, beginning in the Far North, circling counterclockwise around the continent, and ending in the center. It passes through each cultural region, defined centuries ago by ethnologists who wanted to simplify their studies of indigenous peoples. It is my hope that a sampling of oral literature from each region will give children a grander sense of just how many native cultures once thrived here.

Because this is a collection for young children—intended for a younger audience than most retellings of legends of native peoples—I've looked for stories about animals or nature, and avoided those that were too violent or scatological in content. Whenever possible, I tried to keep close to the original telling, but since many of the tales may not have been written down or translated with complete accuracy, it is hard to know for sure how well I have succeeded.

The "teaching" stories gathered here were told for a good reason—they were not meant to be nursery tales created solely for entertainment. Young and old alike listened and learned from them.

My hope is that this book will help children learn too; perhaps they'll come to understand the native peoples' belief that a person is no more important than a beaver or a pine tree or a body of water. Each of us should show respect for all others, for this is essential to keep the earth in balance.

Through hearing the legends, maybe even the youngest will come to know and respect those who first lived in this land. While they listen, I hope they see dancing and hear singing, and imagine the stories being told in a circle, in the dark of winter around a warm fire.

There is a connection to all of those who live in the present, from all of those who lived in the past. In a sense, everything has a way of circling around, again and again.

This may be why native peoples formed circles to relate their stories, to dance and to sing. To them, the circle is the symbol of life. It is the shape of the earth and the sun and the moon. It is the shape of the sacred drum. It is the Medicine Wheel of the Dine and Cheyenne. It is the Sacred Hoop of the Sioux. It is the Sacred Shield of the Crow. It is in a circle that all ceremonies take place.

In a circle, a fire is built.

In a circle, a song is danced.

In a circle, a story is told.

NORTH AMERICA

Because of the nomadic nature of some Native American tribes, their location on this map is general.

1. Inuit
2. Ojibwa
3. Slavey
4. Beaver
5. Duwamish
6. Tlingit
7. Haida
8. Nez Perce
9. Shasta
10. Wishosk
11. Dine
12. Pueblo
13. Creek
14. Cherokee
15. Lenape
16. Seneca
17. Winnebago
18. Pawnee
19. Omaha
20. Sioux
21. Oto

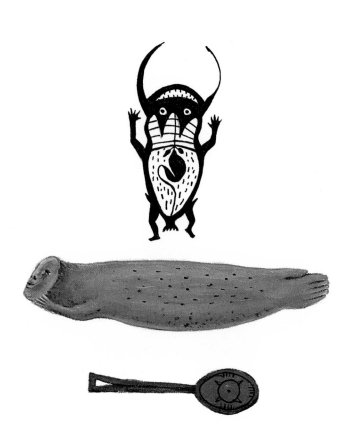

THE ARCTIC

In this frozen land of endless winter nights, where summer visits only for a few short weeks, live the Inuit, or "The People." To the rest of the world, they are known as Eskimo, but Inuit is what they call themselves.

They are a unique race, and are not related to other native peoples who live across the rest of the continent. Though they live in tiny, isolated communities, they speak one language. This has helped them share methods of hunting, toolmaking, and other skills necessary for survival.

They are great storytellers. Telling stories is a way of passing the time during many months of total darkness. Sometimes storytellers challenge each other to see who can stretch the best tale long enough to lull the audience asleep. Some of their stories, such as "Fox Fools Eagle," are about cunning—a very useful trait in such a harsh environment. Their view of a snow-covered "Land in the Sky" makes sense, for that is how their own world looks for most of the year.

Inuit stories are works of art, just as special as their beautiful soapstone carvings of walruses, polar bears, and other creatures that share these frigid waters and barren lands of the Far North.

A STORY!
Inuit (Eskimo)

Grandmother, tell a story, a story!
Grandmother, tell a story!

A story, I do not know it.
Go to sleep, go to snore.

Grandmother, tell a story, a story!
Grandmother, tell a story!

Story! Story! A story before I think of it,
from beneath the house, a little lemming,
a little one without hair will crawl
into your lap, *totutoq,*
and out again, *totutoto!*

FOX FOOLS EAGLE

Inuit (Aleut)

As usual, Fox was hungry.

"I am going to get some eggs," he said, and off he went.

In the middle of the woods, high up in the tallest tree, Fox saw a nest. It belonged to Eagle.

"Hmmm," thought Fox. "I have an idea."

So Fox broke off some grass stalks and stuck them in his ears.

Knock. Knock. Knock. He tapped on the tree with the grass stalks. Eagle looked down.

"Eagle," said Fox, "throw an egg to me."

"No," said Eagle.

14

"If you don't," said Fox, "I will knock the tree over with these stalks!"

Eagle was frightened. He threw down an egg.

"Throw down another," said Fox as he caught the first.

"No," said Eagle.

"If you don't," said Fox, "I will knock over the tree and take *all* your eggs."

Quickly, Eagle threw down another egg.

"Haha-ha!" laughed Fox. "I fooled you! How could I knock down a whole tree with these tiny little grass stalks?"

And off he went.

But Eagle was too angry. Down he flew, grabbed Fox, and lifted him high in the air. Then Eagle flew over glaciers, over mountains, and far out to sea. At last, he set Fox down—on the smallest, loneliest island he could find.

"Now, Fox," said Eagle, "you will not bother anybody ever again." And after taking back his eggs, he left.

Fox circled the island. It did not take long to do.

As he walked round and round, he sang a song:

> "How will I ever get off this island?
> What shall I do? What shall I do?
> *A-he! A-he!*"

Soon the water around the island was full of seals, walruses, and whales, all listening to Fox.

"What is that song you are singing?" they asked. "We could not hear the words."

"Hmmm," thought Fox. "I have an idea."

"This is what I was singing," he said out loud.

> "Which has more animals?
>
> The sea? The sea?
>
> Or the land? The land?
>
> *A-he! A-he!"*

"Certainly there are more animals in the sea," they replied.

"Well, let us see," said Fox. "Come up to the surface and form a raft from this island to the land. Then I will take a walk over you and count you all."

Every whale, walrus, and seal in the sea formed a great raft. And, *fa-whit, fa-whit, fa-whit,* Fox ran over their backs, pretending to count them. As soon as he reached land, he jumped ashore and went home.

That's all!

LAND IN THE SKY
Inuit (Eskimo)

Far away in the land in the sky,
a great chief lives.
In the land in the sky,
a great chief lives in the moon.

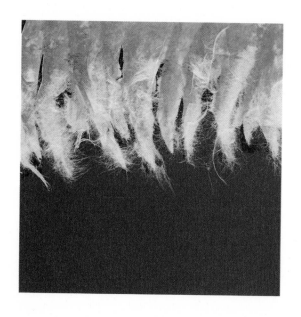

In the land in the sky,
the grass is long.
The long grass grows
down towards earth.
Full of snow,
the grass stems wait for
the wind to come.

In the land in the sky
when the wind blows,
the grass stems sway.
When the grass stems sway,
the snow blows loose
in the land in the sky.
Snow falling downwards,
down towards earth,
is a snowstorm.

In the land in the sky,
there are many round lakes.
In the dark of the night,
these round lakes shine.
The lakes that shine
on earth down below
are stars.

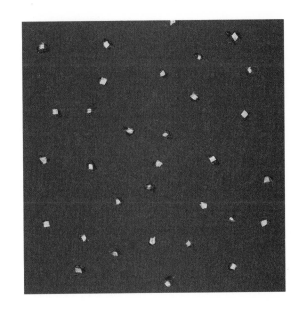

THE SUBARCTIC

The huge Subarctic region stretches over two million square miles, between the coasts of Labrador in the east and Alaska in the west. As in the Arctic, no trees grow in the northern parts—winter lives here for most of the year. The rest is covered with forests and dotted with clear lakes, deep with icy waters.

These lakes are full of wild birds like geese. As long as the hardy creatures have open water to swim in, they don't mind the harsh weather at all. What they do mind are foxes and other animals who like to eat them—as in the tale "Why Fox Is Red."

For most of the animals who live here, even the fox, food is hard to find when the ground is covered with snow. They must face the bitter cold in a struggle to survive. It is no surprise, then, that the Slavey have a legend called "The Long Winter" in which Bear steals all the warmth from the world.

FIREFLY SONG

Ojibwa

Flitting white-fire insects!

Wandering small-fire beasts!

Wave little stars about my bed!

Weave little stars into my sleep!

Come, little dancing white-fire bug!

Come, little flitting white-fire beast!

Light me with your white-flame magic,

Your little star-torch.

THE LONG WINTER
Slavey

There was a time, long ago, when the bears stole the warmth of summer. They took it away to where they lived, far up in the world above. For three years on earth down below, the sun was never seen. The air was dark. Thick gray clouds covered the sky, low to the ground. The snow never stopped, chilling the earth with flakes of white ice. All the animals, including the birds and fish, were freezing and starving to death. So they held a council to decide what to do.

Of course, the animals knew what caused the long winter. They knew that somehow they had to go and get back the warmth that the bears had stolen. And they knew that the journey would not be easy. The narrow opening that led to the upper world was as tiny as the sheaths that held their arrows. Only one animal at a time would be able to pass through it. And the bears may have set some sort of trap at the other end.

Who would go seek the warmth the bears had taken?

It was decided that the seekers of warmth should not be too large.

The seekers of warmth should move quickly and quietly.

The seekers of warmth should have sharp teeth.

At last, Lynx, Fox, Wolf, Wolverine, Mouse, Pike, and Dogfish were chosen for the difficult journey. Together, these friends would travel to the upper world and bring back summer to earth.

Off they went. Pike and Dogfish wriggled through the narrow opening, and Mouse was so tiny, she slipped between its slits in two hops. But Wolf got stuck. Lynx, Fox, and Wolverine pushed and pushed, until finally he was able to slide through. Then, one by one, they pulled themselves up and over to the world above. They were glad that no traps had been set.

Up above, how warm the sun was!

Up above, how beautiful the trees and bushes were!

How refreshing it was to see grass-covered ground, green leaves, and wild berries!

Quickly, silently, they followed the shores of a deep lake until they came to a tipi. A small campfire was burning brightly. So this was where the bears lived!

Next to the fire, two cubs slept soundly. Lynx walked over to the nearest and gave him a gentle nudge.

"Wake up!" said Lynx.

"Awww...Augh!" groaned the little bear. After rubbing the sleep out of his eyes, he woke his brother. "Who are these strange creatures standing beside us?" he whispered.

Fox interrupted. "Where is your mother?"

"She went out hunting," said one.

"But she'll be back very soon!" said the other.

Wolverine and Wolf stepped inside the tipi. There they saw four round, full bags hanging from poles. Immediately, they invited all the others—including the little bears—to join them. Wolf asked, "What's in this bag?"

"That is where our mother keeps the rain," said one cub.

"And what is in this one?" asked Wolverine.

"That is where our mother keeps the wind," said the other.

"And this one?" asked Mouse.

"That is where our mother keeps the fog," said the first.

"And what is in the last bag?" asked Pike and Dogfish.

"Oh," said both together, "it is a secret. Mother would be very angry if we told."

"Don't be afraid," said Wolf. "She won't find out."

"Very well," said the cubs. "That is the bag where she keeps all the heat."

"Ah-h-h-h," said the animals. "This is what we wanted to know."

Wolverine led his friends to the edge of the lake, where the cubs would not be able to hear them. "We must hold a council and decide what to do."

So the animals sat in a circle to think of a plan.

"I know," said Lynx. "I will change myself into a deer and run around to the other side of the lake."

"Good," said Wolf. "The cubs are hungry. Mother Bear will go there to hunt you."

"She will have to use her canoe to cross," said Fox. "That will take a long time."

"Even longer," said Mouse. "For I will gnaw a hole in her paddle!"

"Very wise, little Mouse," said Wolf.

"The rest of us will stay hidden," said Fox. "When Mother Bear leaves, we will grab the bag and carry it back to earth."

They all agreed that this was a good plan and readied themselves to carry it out. Magically, Lynx changed himself into a deer, and followed the long path around to the other side of the lake. Mouse crawled into the bear's canoe and gnawed a deep cut in the paddle. And the others hid.

As soon as the mother bear returned, one of the little cubs cried out, "Mother! Mother, look!" He pointed excitedly. "There's a deer on the other side of the lake!"

"Oh," said Mother Bear, "what a fine dinner we shall have!" Immediately, she jumped into her canoe and set off. But as she paddled faster and faster, *CRACK! SPLASH!* The paddle broke and fell into the water.

THUMP! SPLASH! The bear upset the canoe and fell in too.

"Augh!" cried the cubs.

"Oho!" shouted the animals. "Our plan has worked!"

With their sharp teeth, they quickly cut the lines that held the bag full of heat. Oh, it was heavy! They had to take turns slowly inching the bag towards the opening to the world below.

Since Wolf was the strongest, he pulled first. But soon Wolf said, "I'm too tired." Then Fox and Wolverine tugged and pulled, pushed and shoved.

"Augh!" cried Fox. "Push harder!"

"Look!" squeaked Mouse, peeking over her shoulder. "The mother bear has reached the shore."

"She'll soon catch our deer!" said Wolf, worried about his old friend Lynx.

But just then, Lynx changed back into himself, for he knew that he could run much faster that way.

"Oh, no!" cried Mouse. "Now Mother Bear is heading towards us."

"Hurry!" called Wolf as Dogfish grabbed the bag and pulled.

"We're nearly there," shouted Fox as Lynx caught up to them.

Mother Bear moved closer and closer to the animals. She was about to pounce when Pike flicked his tail, grabbed the bag, and pushed it through the small opening. All of the others jumped to safety, down to the world below.

The bag fell down, then hit the earth. *RIP! WHOOSH!* Out rushed the heat, spreading warmth to all parts of the world. At once, the ice and snow began to melt. All of the animals squealed with delight, for soon the plants would grow and the trees would be green.

For three days, they danced to celebrate the safe return of the seekers of warmth. But on the fourth day, the animals started to worry. Now that all the snow was melting, most of the earth would soon be buried in water. All but the fish and the birds would drown!

To save themselves, some, like Raccoon, Squirrel, and Lynx, scrambled to the highest branches of the tallest tree. But others, like Fox, Wolverine, and Wolf, could not climb trees, so they hurried to the top of a great mountain. And from the

corners of the earth, all of the animals cried out, "Help! Help! Help!"

Out of nowhere appeared an enormous water creature with magnificent fins, speckled scales, and a huge mouth, opened wide. It began to drink the water. As it drank, its huge body swelled up, until all the floodwaters were gone.

Soon the earth was dry, the dark clouds moved away, and for the first time in three years, the sun appeared. Trees and

bushes once again covered themselves with fresh green leaves and luscious berries. Now there would be plenty to eat and the animals would at last be warm.

From that time forth, winter has stayed only as long as it is needed. The animals are content, for now they have heat and the warm sun to look forward to as summer returns, year after year. Since that time of the long winter, the earth has been just as it is today.

WHY FOX IS RED

Beaver

Fox was very hungry.

Loppita–loppita–loppita went Fox, uphill, downhill, all around the countryside, looking for something to eat.

At the edge of a lake, he saw a goose with her flock of babies. He ran after them and as he ran, he sang:

> "I shall have your
> tender meat
> before I go to sleep.
> I shall have your
> tender meat before
> I go to sleep."

As soon as Fox ran towards the geese, they plunged into the water. *Loppita–loppita–loppita* went Fox, back and forth, back and forth, along the edge of the water. Farther and farther away swam the geese. Angrier and angrier grew Fox. Soon the geese were floating in the middle of the lake. Fox howled: *"AAAHOOOOHHHHH!"* But he could not catch them. Fox was so angry, he turned red all over— except for the tip of his tail. And to this day, he has stayed that way.
So it is told.

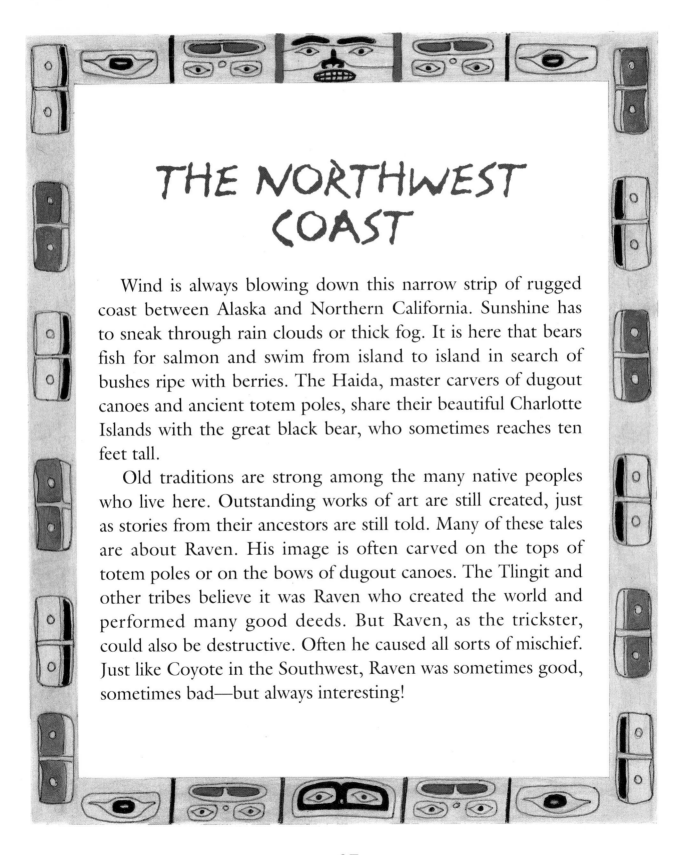

THE NORTHWEST COAST

Wind is always blowing down this narrow strip of rugged coast between Alaska and Northern California. Sunshine has to sneak through rain clouds or thick fog. It is here that bears fish for salmon and swim from island to island in search of bushes ripe with berries. The Haida, master carvers of dugout canoes and ancient totem poles, share their beautiful Charlotte Islands with the great black bear, who sometimes reaches ten feet tall.

Old traditions are strong among the many native peoples who live here. Outstanding works of art are still created, just as stories from their ancestors are still told. Many of these tales are about Raven. His image is often carved on the tops of totem poles or on the bows of dugout canoes. The Tlingit and other tribes believe it was Raven who created the world and performed many good deeds. But Raven, as the trickster, could also be destructive. Often he caused all sorts of mischief. Just like Coyote in the Southwest, Raven was sometimes good, sometimes bad—but always interesting!

THE WIND SONG

Duwamish

As wind comes along,

all the pines sing.

The wind comes slowly, slowly

and the pines sing softly, softly,

and wind sings with them

so softly, the wind song.

You can hear it, softly, softly,

as the pines dance, back and forth,

back and forth,

swinging their long arms,
swaying with the song,
singing, singing,
in the language of the pines,
wild and mournful.
The wind calls to the rain:
Come out of the clouds,
sing with us!
The rain dances madly with the wind,
riding down, resting on the pines.
The pines bending, bending,
their needles brush the grass.
Shhh…listen!
Can you hear them?

RAVEN, THE RIVER MAKER
Tlingit

At first, the animals had no fresh water, no water at all to drink. The water on earth was filled with salt, and the animals were thirsty. Raven was thirsty too.

With feathers white as clouds, Raven floated above earth, searching for water to drink.

Just like a cloud, Raven could move about wherever he pleased, unnoticed by anyone.

Even Wolf did not see Raven as he passed over his tiny island. But Raven saw Wolf.

Raven saw Wolf fill buckets of fresh water from his well.

Raven saw Wolf carry buckets of fresh water to his house. Raven saw that all the fresh water on earth belonged to Wolf. So this was why the other animals had no fresh water, no water at all to drink! Raven flew down.

Wolf, glad to have company, invited Raven to spend the night.

This is just what Raven wanted him to do.

Soon it was dark. When Wolf fell asleep, Raven tiptoed over to the buckets of fresh water. How thirsty he was!

Raven drank until all the buckets were empty. Raven drank up all the fresh water in the world.

Wolf woke up. He saw that his buckets were empty. He saw Raven fly up the smoke hole to escape.

But Raven, fat and swollen, full of water, got stuck!

Wolf lit a fire of green wood. Thick smoke quickly rose up and darkened Raven's feathers. Now Raven was black like the night of no moon.

When Raven escaped, drops of water dripped off his feathers as he soared high above land. Each drop of water became a river. Each river split into other rivers and small streams.

Now, thanks to Raven, the thirsty animals all over earth at last have fresh water to drink.

Is that so? Yes, that is so.

NO FROGS AT ALL
Haida

Once, long ago, an island frog, jumping through wild flowers, came upon a narrow trail and decided to see where it went. As the frog hop-hopped down this path, he met a huge bear, a giant bear that was ten feet tall, who said, "You ugly little brute! What are you doing in my way?"

The frog was so scared, he could not answer.

The bear picked him up, smelled him, turned him round and round, then set him down again, growling, "You dirty little brute! You are too ugly for me!"

And the huge bear, the giant bear that was ten feet tall, went off.

The frog hop-hopped home as fast as he could, telling everyone he saw, "*Garrumph!* There's a terrible monster in

44

the woods! We must get rid of him before he kills us all! *Garrumph-garrumph!*"

So the frogs on the island quickly gathered together to listen.

"*Garrumph!*" said the little frog. "He called me a brute!"

"*Ewww!*" gasped the frogs, trembling with terror.

"*Garrumph!*" said the little frog. "He picked me up with his mighty claws!"

"*EW-EW-EWWW!*" shrieked the others as they turned pale green with fear.

"*Garrumph!*" said the little frog. "He turned me round and round, then stuck his huge, black, wet nose in my face and sniffed!"

"*EW-EW-EW-EWWW!*" they all howled together, and fell over, all at once, nearly dead from fright.

At last, one said weakly, "We must do something."

"But what?" replied the others.

"Maybe we should learn how to climb up a very tall tree," said the first.

"*Humph!*" said the eldest. "Frogs don't climb trees!"

"Then perhaps we should try to fly away," said another.

"*Humph!*" said the elder frog. "Have you ever seen a frog fly?"

"We could dig a hole and hide," suggested the youngest.

"*Garrumph!*" said the eldest. "What do you think we are? Moles with sharp claws?"

Before long, they concluded that there was not much they could do.

The bear was too fierce. It was useless to try to kill it.

The bear was too big. It was useless to try to drive it away.

So the frogs did the only thing they could think of doing. They left.

That is why there are no frogs living on the Charlotte Islands today.

This is true, so they say.

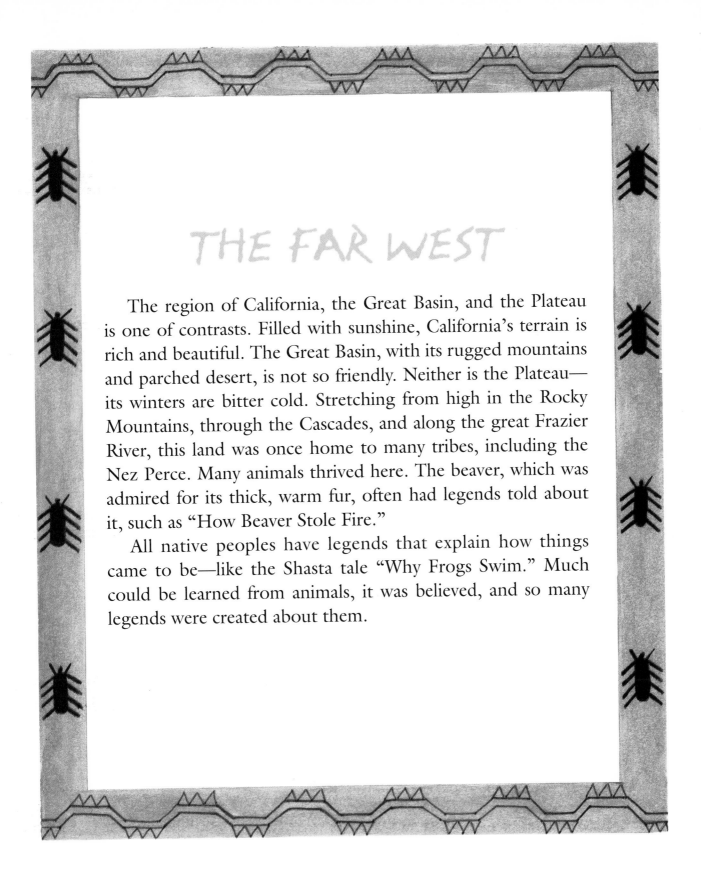

THE FAR WEST

The region of California, the Great Basin, and the Plateau is one of contrasts. Filled with sunshine, California's terrain is rich and beautiful. The Great Basin, with its rugged mountains and parched desert, is not so friendly. Neither is the Plateau— its winters are bitter cold. Stretching from high in the Rocky Mountains, through the Cascades, and along the great Frazier River, this land was once home to many tribes, including the Nez Perce. Many animals thrived here. The beaver, which was admired for its thick, warm fur, often had legends told about it, such as "How Beaver Stole Fire."

All native peoples have legends that explain how things came to be—like the Shasta tale "Why Frogs Swim." Much could be learned from animals, it was believed, and so many legends were created about them.

HOW BEAVER STOLE FIRE
Nez Perce

Long before there were people, animals and trees talked to each other and moved about—just as people do today.

At this time, the pine trees, who always kept to themselves, had a great secret they did not wish to share. Not with anyone. It was *fire*. When icy winds blew, the pine trees would huddle around their secret to keep warm, *and* to hide it. Meanwhile, all the other trees and animals shivered and trembled, for they had no such magic.

One year, there came a long, long winter that refused to go away. Animals and trees everywhere were freezing to death. This was the winter that Beaver discovered the great secret of the pines.

It happened like this: One icy cold day, Beaver was fishing in the Grande Ronde River in Idaho. Near the banks, he saw a great circle of pine trees. He watched as some of the pines made their way down to the icy water, jumped in to bathe, then quickly ran back to the center of the circle.

Sneaking closer, Beaver saw a huge fire. The pines were standing around it, warm and dry.

When Beaver saw that the tallest pines were guarding the fire, he understood. Those unfriendly pines wanted to keep

this great magic all for themselves! He crawled under the banks and hid.

Suddenly the fire crackled. The fire popped. A live coal burst out of the flames and rolled down the riverbank right in front of Beaver's hiding place.

At once, Beaver grabbed it and tucked the hot coal inside his thick fur. *Oph!* It was burning! He ran off as quickly and quietly as he could.

But a guard saw Beaver and cried out, "Stop, thief!" Immediately, all of the other pine trees took off after him.

At first, Beaver was able to run in a straight line. But as the pines got closer, he began to zigzag this way and that to escape them. The Grande Ronde River, who disliked secrets of any kind, wanted to teach the pine trees a lesson. To help Beaver, the river followed his roundabout path and blocked the pine trees. And that is the way it still flows today.

The pines soon grew tired, for they had only fat trunks, not

legs to run with like Beaver. One by one, they tripped and fell, tripped and fell, as their roots caught on the scraggly brush. All but the tallest finally gave up. They stopped, up, down, and around the riverbanks. And that is exactly where they stand today.

But the great cedar kept running. He did not want the other trees and animals to learn about fire. He alone understood its tremendous power. He knew that fire could be used unwisely. Cedar, of course, was right, for today fire is one of the greatest enemies of all trees.

So Cedar called out to the others, "I will go to the top of the hill and see how far ahead Beaver is."

He reached the top just in time to see Beaver dive into the Big Snake River, right where the Grande Ronde now enters it. He saw Beaver swim across and give fire to the willows, then cross back again to give fire to the birches, then far, far down the river, to give fire to some of the other trees. And he saw these trees become the givers of fire by rubbing the sticks of their branches just so, to create new fire.

The great cedar also saw that there was nothing more he could do. Beaver had stolen fire. Every animal and tree would soon know this secret. Now all who wanted fire would be told how to rub willow and birch or other sticks together in a special way. They would be able to create a fire of their own.

So the tallest pine tree finally gave up too. Today that great old cedar, his top now dead, still stands all alone on the hill where the Big Snake River meets the Grande Ronde. There are no other cedars within a hundred miles upstream from where he stands. Every animal who passes by points at that tree and remembers Beaver.

So far goes the story.

WHY FROGS SWIM

Shasta

Once in the long-ago time, when frogs lived only on land, Snake saw Frog and his little ones playing games, leaping, hopping, jumping this way and that, near the edge of a river.

As Snake crawled along, one little frog hopped over him. Snake coiled up in disgust. *"Hssss!"*

56

Snake sniffed. "*Hssss! Puh!* You smell terrible!"

"What did you say?" the big frog asked.

"I said your child stinks!" said Snake. "Don't you ever bathe him?"

"No," Frog answered.

"Don't you ever take him for a swim?" Snake asked.

"Never," Frog said.

"Well," said Snake, hissing loudly, "no wonder he stinks!"

Snake slithered off.

Frog thought for a moment, then hopped over to where his child was playing, picked him up, and threw him in the river.

Kerplunk! SPLASH!

A little while later, Snake came back.

"Where is your child?" he asked.

"I threw him in the river," Frog answered.

"But," Snake said, "that is not what I told you to do. I said you should *bathe* your child."

"Well," said Frog, "he is in the river now. Let him stay there."

With that, Frog hopped off.

To this day, frogs live in the water and know how to swim. And since they no longer smell so bad, snakes eat them whenever they can.

HOW SPIDER CAUGHT FLIES
Wishosk

When the Great Maker first put Spider on earth, Spider wished to eat flies but had no way to catch them. He had no wings to fly like a bird. He had no long, sticky tongue like a lizard. All he had was a tiny mouth with no teeth, and legs that were much too long and delicate.

"What good is this mouth?" said Spider. "All I can use it for is talking, since I have nothing to eat."

Then Spider said, "What good are these legs? Besides walking, running, or hopping, what can I use them for?"

So Spider sat very still and watched flies *BZZ BZZ BZZ* this way and that.

He grew hungrier and hungrier.

Finally, he could stand it no longer. He called out to the Great Maker for his help. "Oh, Old Man Above," Spider said, "I want to eat flies! But, *o-o-o-pa-a-a!* I have no way to catch them."

Old Man Above listened, then said, "Spider, here is some string. Why don't you sit here for a while and work with it."

Spider was puzzled. What good would a piece of thin string do?

By now, Spider was starving. He put some of this string into his mouth and swallowed. Old Man Above saw Spider do this, but said nothing. Spider was so hungry, he swallowed and swallowed, more and more, until soon his huge belly was stuffed full of string.

But still he felt hungry!

As Spider sat there with the end of the string hanging out of his mouth, a sudden storm approached. *Pit-pat-pit-pat!* Rain fell all about him.

"I hate rain," cried Spider, shivering. "*Brrr!* I don't want to get wet!"

RUMBLE RUMBLE BOOM! Thunder roared, lightning flashed.

"I hate thunder and lightning," said Spider, shaking. "*Brrrr!* I want to go down, way down beneath this cliff where it is dry and safe."

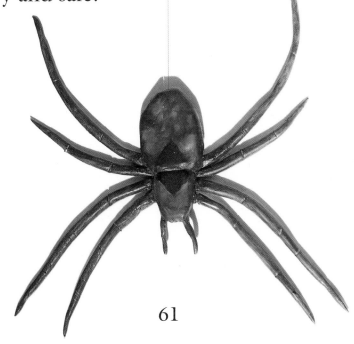

But then he had an idea. "*Ho!* I know what I'll do!"

He pulled the end of the string from his mouth, tied it to a branch, and slowly, slowly let himself down.

Now Spider was dry and happy! He let out more string. Round he went, weaving the string, in and out, in and out.

Soon he'd created a beautiful design, shaped like a star. He sat down in the middle of it to rest.

BUZZZZ! A fly flew by. *OHO!* It was caught in the string and couldn't get out!

At last, Spider had found a way to catch flies! With his long, nimble legs, he scrambled over to the fly, spat out more string, and quickly wrapped it up—and bit by bit, *CHOMP! CHOMP! CHOMP!* Spider gobbled it all up.

THE SOUTHWEST

Some of the largest nations of native people in North America, including the Dine (Navajo), Hopi, and Pueblo, call this region home. Here the weather can be very cold, especially at night, or very hot when the sun is shining. Since much of the area is dry desert and rain is hardly ever seen, many native peoples include rain dances as part of their rituals. Through irrigation, they are able to grow crops of corn—their staple food.

This is the land of the Grand Canyon, the Painted Desert, cactus, roadrunners, and of course, coyotes. Probably more stories have been told about Coyote than any other animal.

The ultimate trickster hero, Coyote can do just about anything he puts his mind to. The Crow say that Coyote created the world. That was a good thing. The Apache say that Coyote released all the buffalo to roam free over the Great Plains. That was good too. But sometimes, Coyote acts a little bit foolish. His curiosity gets him into all kinds of trouble, as in the Tewa legend told here.

THE CORN SONG

Dine (Navajo)

With this it grows, with this it grows,
the dark cloud, with this it grows.
The dew thereof, with this it grows,
the blue corn, with this it grows.

This it eats, this it eats,
the dark cloud.
Its dew
the blue corn eats.
This it eats.

The great corn plant is with the bean,*
its roots now are with the bean,
its leaf tips now are with the bean,
its dewdrops now are with the bean,
its tassel now is with the bean,

bean blossom

its pollen now is with the bean,
and now its silk is with the bean,
and now its grain is with the bean.

The corn grows up. The waters of the dark clouds
drop, drop.
The rain descends. The waters from the corn leaves
drop, drop.
The rain descends. The waters from the plants
drop, drop.
The corn grows up. The waters of the dark mists
drop, drop.

Shall I pick this fruit
of the great corn plant?
Shall you break it? Shall I break it?
Shall I break it? Shall you break it?
Shall I? Shall you?

COYOTE AND THE BLACKBIRDS
Pueblo (Tewa)

Coyote was walking along, *loppa loppa lop, loppa loppa lop,* feeling pleased and proud of himself as usual.

Just then, he heard: *KEOW! KEOW! Flutter, flutter, flap!*

Coyote stopped.

He looked up. Blackbirds!

Flitta-flitting here, *flitta-flitting* there, the blackbirds were chattering excitedly.

Coyote cocked his head and listened.

"*KEOW! KEOW!* It's going to hail! It's going to hail!" they called.

Coyote moved closer.

"Bring me my bag! Bring me my bag!" said one.

"It's going to hail! It's going to hail!" called another.

Coyote looked at the sky. It was a clear, deep blue.

"What are you talking about?" asked Coyote.

"Too busy to talk, too busy to talk," they chattered.

"What is wrong with all of you?" asked Coyote.

"Just you wait, just you wait," they said.

Coyote sat down. He yawned. He watched. He waited. He yawned again.

As the blackbirds sang, *"KEOW! KEOW!"* they hung buckskin bags from the branches of the tallest tree.

All this fuss made Coyote nervous. He began to pace back and forth, back and forth, *lop loppa loppa lop, lop loppa loppa lop.*

"Maybe these blackbirds know something I don't," thought Coyote.

Loppa loppa lop. Loppa loppa lop.

"Maybe there's a good reason why they are hanging bags in the trees."

Loppa loppa lop. Loppa loppa lop.

Coyote stood on his hind legs and called out: *"HA-HAY-OOO!* Whatever it is that you are doing, I want to do, too!"

Coyote hated to be left out of anything.

The blackbirds seemed pleased.

"Oh, friend Coyote," they called sweetly, "we would love for you to join us."

"Good!" said Coyote, feeling much better now. "Tell me," he said, "what exactly are you doing with those bags?"

"Oh, friend Coyote," said the blackbirds, "we shall hide inside them. When it hails, we won't be pelted to death."

"What a good idea!" said Coyote. "May I join you?"

"Oh, yes! Oh, yes!" chirped the blackbirds. "Good idea! Good idea!"

Quickly, Coyote ran home, found a large bag just his size, and brought it back to the blackbirds, who were waiting.

"Just right! Just right!" called the blackbirds, trying hard not to laugh.

"Get in, get in!" they said.

Coyote climbed inside the bag. The blackbirds flew down.

"Tie the rope! Tie the rope!" said one.

"Pull it up! Pull it up!" said another.

Soon Coyote, inside the bag, was pulled high above the ground, where he swung back and forth, back and forth, from the branch of the tallest tree.

The blackbirds, full of mischief, gathered pebbles from the ground.

"KEOW! KEOW!" they called excitedly. "Here comes the storm! Here comes the hail!" Then they threw stones at the swinging bag as hard as they could.

"Mercy, oh, mercy!" yelled Coyote. "What a terrible storm it is indeed!"

"KEE-KEEOW!" chirped the blackbirds as they pelted Coyote.

"Ouch!" said Coyote. "Thank goodness I'm safe inside this bag!"

"KAYAI! KAYAI!" cried the blackbirds, pretending to suffer as they threw pebbles at the bag.

"*OW! OW!*" howled Coyote. "If it hurts me like this, it must really hurt you!"

"Yes, yes!" cried the blackbirds. "It hurts us much more

than it hurts you, friend Coyote." Then they pelted the bag again, even harder this time.

"OUCH!" yelled Coyote. "That one nearly hit my eye!"

"Be brave, be brave, friend Coyote," crooned the blackbirds. "You are much stronger than we are." They pelted him as hard as they could.

"OW! OW! OWOOOOO!" yelled Coyote.

The blackbirds were too tired to throw anymore. They untied the rope and slowly, slowly let the bag down to the ground. As soon as the bag opened up, they rushed to the top of the tree.

"Ohhh..." groaned Coyote, crawling out, so bruised and sore he could barely move. "I think I am dead," he said.

Coyote lay quite still for a while, then opened his eyes and looked around.

What? The sun was shining!

What? There were no clouds in the sky!

What? The ground was dry! There were no hailstones anywhere!

"AUGH! AUGHHH! What a mean trick you have played on me!" Coyote groaned as the blackbirds, laughing and cackling, flew over his head, just out of reach.

Coyote limped home in a terrible rage as the blackbirds followed, teasing and taunting him.

"AUGH! I'll eat you all!" he growled.

"You can't catch us! You can't catch us!" they screamed.

But the next day, he did.

And from that time forth, blackbird stew became Coyote's favorite dinner.

This is how war on this earth first began.

Is that so? Yes, that is so.

THE MOCKINGBIRD SONG

Pueblo (Tigua)

Rain, people, rain!
Rain all around us.
Come pouring down,
then summer will be fair to see.
The mockingbird has said so.
Hi-ni-ni! A-hi-ni-ni!
A-ni-a! A-ha-i-hi!

THE SOUTHEAST

The land that stretches from the Atlantic Ocean all the way down to the Gulf of Mexico and up to the valleys of Ohio was once home to many different native peoples. The mysterious architecture of the Adena, known as "The Mound Builders," can still be seen in Ohio. In the mountains of Appalachia lived the Cherokee, with their own alphabet and system of writing. Farther south, in Georgia and Alabama, were the Creek, who knew the secrets of certain plants used in medicines today.

The Cherokee are known for their wonderful animal stories. The one told here is about Possum, who dangles from hickory limbs in this region. The legends of the Creek Nation are the best "artifacts" we have of their culture, which was destroyed by whites during the "Indian Wars" of the 1800s. They help explain the Creek way of life, their beliefs and history. Many of their stories closely resemble African tales, particularly those about Rabbit, like "A Tug of War." It is hard to know exactly where or when these stories first came to be. Maybe way back in the beginning, there was just one storyteller, and through time, his tales spread all over the world!

MOTHER SUN
Creek (Yuchi)

Who will make the light?
it was said, it was said.
I will make the light,
Yohah, the Star, said.

So it was agreed.

The Star shone forth.

A circle of light,

a small circle of light,

only around the Star.

Who will make more light?

it was said, it was said.

I will make more light,

Shar-pah, the Moon, said.

The Moon made more light,

but it was still dark,

so dark.

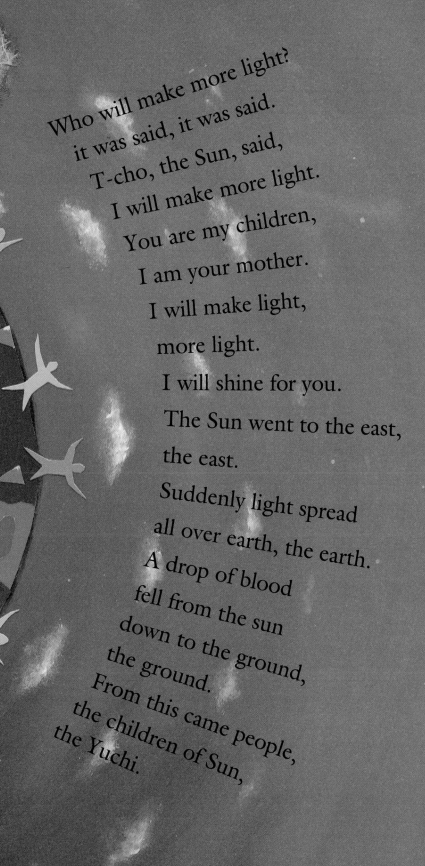

Who will make more light?
it was said, it was said.
T-cho, the Sun, said,
I will make more light.
You are my children,
I am your mother.
I will make light,
more light.
I will shine for you.
The Sun went to the east,
the east.
Suddenly light spread
all over earth, the earth.
A drop of blood
fell from the sun
down to the ground,
the ground.
From this came people,
the children of Sun,
the Yuchi.

A TUG OF WAR
Creek (Taskigi)

One day, Rabbit was hip-hopping along when suddenly he heard a loud *SSSSSSSSSSSSSSSS!* Rabbit stopped. He lifted his head, twitched his nose, *sniff, sniff, sniff!*...and found himself face to face with Tie Snake, the strongest beast in the land.

"Humph!" thought Rabbit. "I don't care how strong he is. I bet I can fool him." So he followed Tie Snake, whose short, thick tail whipped side to side, side to side, as he slithered towards his den.

Rabbit went *hippity-hoppity, hippity-hoppity,* right beside Tie Snake, who did not like it at all, not at all. He said, *"SSSSSSSSSSSS!* Rabbit, go home. Leave me alone."

"I'll go, I'll go," said Rabbit. "But before I go, I want to challenge you to a contest."

"*SSSSSSSSSSSS!* What kind of contest?" asked Tie Snake, weaving side to side, side to side.

"A pulling contest," said Rabbit, hipping and hopping up and down excitedly.

"Ha!" said Tie Snake. "Between whom?"

"You and me," said Rabbit.

"*SSSSSSSSSSSS!*" said Tie Snake, coiling into a tight ball. "You're much too small. You'll lose."

"Just meet me at the river's edge, four days from today," said Rabbit. "And we'll see who the strongest puller is." With that, Rabbit hopped off, leaving Tie Snake looking puzzled, very puzzled indeed.

Rabbit crossed over to the other side, the other side of the river, where he found another tie snake, breathing in, breathing out, sunning himself on a log.

"Oh, friend Tie Snake!" said Rabbit, hipping and hopping up and down excitedly.

"*SSSSSSSSSSSS!*" said Tie Snake. "Rabbit, go home! Leave me alone."

"I'll go, I'll go," said Rabbit. "But before I go, I want to challenge you to a contest."

"*SSSSSSSSSSSS!* What kind of contest?" asked Tie Snake, twisting and turning, turning and twisting, over and under the log.

"A pulling contest," said Rabbit, tweaking his whiskers and twitching his nose excitedly.

"Ha!" said Tie Snake. "Between whom?"

"You and me," said Rabbit.

"SSSSSSSSSSS!" said Tie Snake, rolling into a wide hoop. "You're much too small. You'll lose."

"Just meet me at the river's edge, four days from today," said Rabbit. "And we'll see who the strongest puller is!"

Rabbit hopped off, leaving this tie snake looking every bit as puzzled as the first one.

Now Rabbit found a great big grapevine, untangled it, stretched it and pulled it, then laid one end on one side of the river and the other end on the opposite side. Each contestant would have to pick up his end and pull with all his might. "Whoever lands in the river first, loses," laughed

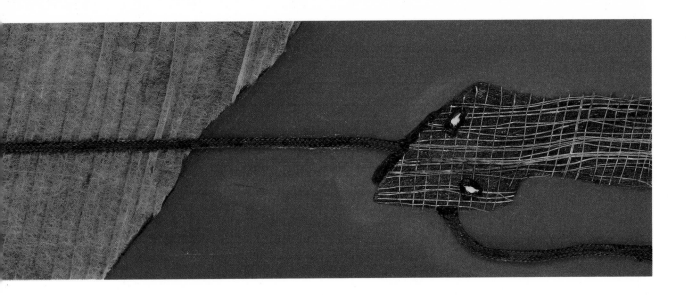

Rabbit. "And, *hee hee hee!* It won't be me!"

Early on the fourth morning, Rabbit hid himself in the brush beside the river. Along came the tie snakes, who did not see each other, not at all. On opposite sides of the river, each took hold of the grapevine.

Rabbit whooped, "Yes! Yes! Start pulling!"

Both tie snakes, thinking Rabbit was at the other end, gave a big yank. *OOMPH!* Nothing happened. They yanked again and again. *OOMPH! OOMPH!* Still nothing. This time, they were angry, really angry, so they pulled and pulled with all their might. *OOMPH! OOMPH! OOMPH!* Nothing. All day long, long into the night, they yanked and pulled, pulled and yanked, while Rabbit laughed and laughed, until he could laugh no more, and finally fell asleep.

When he woke up the next day, the tie snakes were still at it.

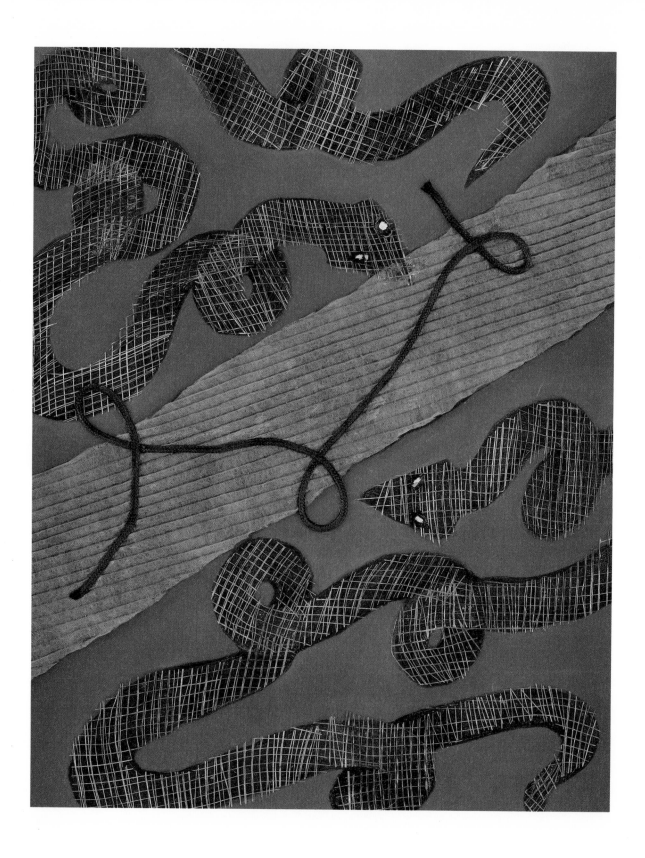

They looked terrible. Ragged and beaten, they no longer looked like the strongest beasts in the land. Like the grapevine, they were doubled up in knots.

"Let's have a rest," called Rabbit. "We'll meet back here tomorrow and begin again." Immediately, both snakes let go and dragged themselves wearily back to their dens.

The following morning, bright and early, Rabbit went *hippity-hoppity, hippity-hoppity* over to the first tie snake, who said, "*SSSSSSSSSSSS!* Rabbit, go home! Leave me alone."

"Why, what's the matter, friend Tie Snake?" asked Rabbit.

"I'm much too tired to pull. You win."

Then Rabbit went *hippity-hoppity, hippity-hoppity* over to the other Tie Snake, who said, "*SSSSSSSSSSSS!* Rabbit, go home! Leave me alone!"

"Why, whatever is the matter, friend Tie Snake?" asked Rabbit.

"You are the strongest beast in this land," he said. "You win."

Because Rabbit fooled the tie snakes, they respected him and called him their friend. They even allowed Rabbit the privilege of going to the river to get his water, instead of having to go to wells like the others.

This is for true.

HOW POSSUM GOT HIS SKINNY TAIL

Cherokee

In the old days, Possum had the most beautiful tail of all the animals. He was so proud, oh, so proud! Each day, he would strut about, *heh-heh-hah, heh-heh-hah,* flicking his long, silky tail back and forth, round and about, showing it off to all of the other animals.

"Oh, isn't this tail, this wonderful tail, the most beautiful, beautiful, beautiful tail you have ever seen?" he would say. "Watch me swing it back and forth, round and about, so!" *Sweesh! Sweesh!* "I am certain that its color, its *silver* color, its *shiny* silver color, is unlike any other in the world!"

It wasn't long before the other animals grew tired of hearing Possum talk about his fine tail. And it was Rabbit who finally decided to teach him a lesson.

Rabbit called on Possum and invited him to come to a council meeting.

"Please join us, friend Possum," Rabbit said. "Our chief, Bear, insists that you sit next to him and wants you to be the first to speak, for you have the most beautiful tail."

Of course Possum agreed. "Well, if he really wants me to,

then I suppose I should. It is true that my tail is the most beautiful," he said.

"Perhaps I should get a closer look at it, friend Possum," said Rabbit. "Turn around."

Delighted to show off his tail to Rabbit, Possum did as he was told.

"Hmmm..." said Rabbit. "I'm afraid it looks a bit dirty."

Possum whirled around and examined it closely. Although he didn't see anything wrong, he couldn't be certain. "Are you sure?"

"Quite sure," said Rabbit.

"Oh, my!" said Possum. "What shall I do?"

"Don't worry," said Rabbit. "I'll be happy to clean it for you."

"Oh, friend Rabbit," said Possum, "I am much obliged to you for taking the time to do so."

Quickly, Rabbit mixed up a potion, rubbed it all over Possum's tail, then wrapped a dried snakeskin tightly around it like a bandage.

"Now, friend Possum, whatever you do, don't remove this snakeskin until you are ready to speak at the council meeting. The snakeskin has magic powers. It will make this potion do wonders for your beautiful tail."

"Very well," said Possum. "I promise."

All that night, Possum dreamed long dreams. He dreamed of how his clean, soft, glimmering tail would cause the whole council to stand up and stomp in admiration. Why, the meeting probably wouldn't get under way until the end of the day, for everyone would beg him to strut up and down, back and forth, round and about.

Possum could hardly wait for morning to arrive. When it did, he scurried off and was the first animal, besides Bear, to arrive at the council meeting. Proudly, he took his seat right next to Bear, who was a little surprised, but said nothing.

As soon as all the animals had gathered, Possum jumped up so that he would be the first to speak. Right off, he removed the snakeskin and began to saunter back and forth, round and about, very proudly—to show off his magnificent, clean tail. "Oh, isn't this tail, this wonderful tail, the most beautiful,

beautiful, beautiful tail you have ever seen? Watch me swing it back and forth, round and about, so!" *Sweesh! Sweesh!*

But when the other animals saw it, they fell over laughing and howling.

"Look how it glistens!" said Possum proudly. "Watch how its silver color sparkles as it moves!" *Sweesh! Sweesh!*

All of the animals were now rolling across the ground, shouting, "Ugly! Ugly!"

Possum stood still. "What are you talking about?"

Squirrel pointed. "What are *you* talking about?" Then everybody laughed some more.

Possum turned around and looked for himself.

"Oh, no!" cried Possum. "Where is my tail? Where is my beautiful tail?"

Well, his tail was still there, but it had no hair.

"It's bald! It's completely bald!" cried Possum.

Now the other animals began to parade about, delighted to show off their own tails.

"Look at my beautiful, long, full tail," said Squirrel. "Look as I make it go back and forth, round and about." *Sweesh! Sweesh!*

"Oh, look at mine," said Fox. "How fine and red and wonderful it is!" *Sweesh! Sweesh!*

"Ohhh...AUGH!" howled Possum as he fell to the ground and hid his head, so embarrassed! So ashamed! He pretended to be dead.

Long after the meeting was over, long after all of the other animals had gone home, Possum still lay on the ground, motionless. He did not dare get up until early the next morning while the others, he knew, would still be sleeping. Then, *zip-zip-zip!*—he scurried up to the top of the tall tree where he lived, and hung there, upside down, for the rest of the day.

And we know that Possum, when threatened, always pretends to be dead. And each day, all the day long, he hangs upside down in a tree to sleep, for that is the only good thing he can do with his ugly tail.

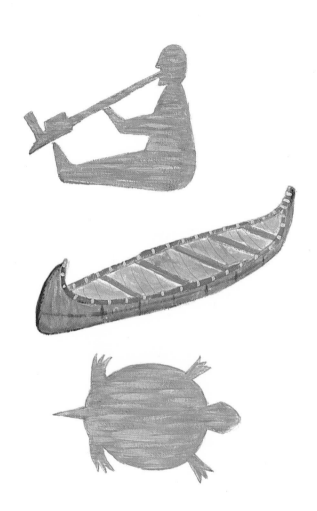

THE NORTHEAST

From above Lake Superior, west to the Mississippi, east to the Atlantic coast, all the way down to what is now Tennessee, great hunters, farmers, and fishermen once lived. These were the most powerful and sophisticated nations of native peoples north of Mexico. Their beautiful land was covered with forest and filled with nuts and berries, so food was plentiful. The many birds and animals of all kinds were woven into their wonderful legends, as in "Rabbit and the Willow." Even the creation of earth involved the help of various animals like Turtle, Muskrat, and Beaver.

These native peoples gave much to those who came from across the Atlantic. Words such as *moose, moccasin, woodchuck, skunk,* and *hickory* come from their languages. The Lenape were among those who taught the early settlers how to plant corn, squash, and other foods, and showed them how to net fish in the rivers and cook shellfish from the sea. Even the formation of our democracy and the United States Constitution was based on the structure of the League of Six Nations founded by the great Iroquois.

Lenape

In the beginning, when Great Spirit created Earth, our mother,
there was no land. Just water. Then Great Spirit sent Turtle
to Earth. His shell was smooth and bright yellow like the
sun. Turtle swam and swam, but soon grew tired, for
there was no place to rest. Great Spirit sent Muskrat
and Beaver to Earth. They swam and swam,
but when they grew tired, they
rested on Turtle's back.

So Great Spirit told Muskrat
and Beaver to dive down to the bottom,
bring up mud, and pile it on Turtle's back. They
did what they were told, and this became the first land.
Turtle's back was now stained black except for where Muskrat
and Beaver left their footprints. These were bright yellow like
the moon and stars. The land began to grow. Soon Turtle was
able to slip from beneath and crawl up on top to rest. After a long
while, Great Spirit placed other animals on Earth. Birds flew above
and fish swam in the waters below. *This is how it all came to be.*

RABBIT AND THE WILLOW
Seneca

Do you know what our friend Gwa-io, the rabbit, once looked like? He did not look like Rabbit at all! Not at all! His ears were like twigs, his tail like a bush! What's more, those legs of his were just four long sticks, all the same size. But like Rabbit, he loved to nibble tender green leaves and run, *ti-wit-ta, ti-wit-ta,* in the early morning sun.

Once Rabbit was running about, *ti-wit-ta, ti-wit-ta,* when a thick blanket of clouds crossed the sun and the air suddenly grew cold. Great North Wind howled, *"A-gee! A-gee!"* teasing Earth with its icy breath.

Round and round Rabbit kept running in a great big circle, when something that looked like the soft down of wintering geese began to fall from the sky.

So Rabbit ran faster and faster, singing as he ran:

"*Ah-gah-nee-ya-ah-yenh!*

When it snows,

how I run about,

when it snows!"

Snow fell quickly, thickly swirling round and round Rabbit as he sang, *"Ah-gah-nee-ya-ah-yenh!"* all the day long.

When Rabbit stopped running, Snow stopped falling. Now, a thick white blanket covered the tender green leaves, bending the branches of the tall willow tree close to the ground.

It was here that Rabbit, exhausted, soon bedded down, quietly singing:

"It was I who brought Snow,

brought Snow,

running, running round so."

Then he fell sound asleep, shaded by the pale smile of Soi-ka Gaa-kwa, the half moon. Half Moon was smiling because she knew that Snow had tricked Rabbit.

While he slept, Daga-e-da, Great South Wind, whistled a soft tune, *"Whe-ish...whe-ish..."* and warmed up Earth. This caused a sudden thaw.

Poor Rabbit did not know that he was sleeping on a willow branch, for Snow hid it. So the next day, when Rabbit woke up, Snow was gone, but he was way, way, way up above the ground!

"Kwe!" shrieked Rabbit. "How did I get up here? Rabbits don't climb trees!" He knew he was too high up to jump, so he sat very still. As Rabbit sat, he grew hungrier and hungrier. Looking down, seeing the tender green grass made him even hungrier, but *oh, no!* He was not going to jump. He was going to stay just where he was and sit very still.

A dark shadow, no

100

larger than a speck of dust, passed high above the ground. As it looked down, it spied Rabbit sitting in the tree.

Circling closer and closer, the shadow grew into a magnificent hawk, with wings as long as the branch of the tall willow where Rabbit sat very still.

With claws outstretched, Hawk swooped down, singing excitedly, *"Hai! Haiiii!"* and...POUNCED!

But luckily for Rabbit, he missed. His great wings just jiggled the branch, and off bounced Rabbit!

Down, down fell Rabbit. *Kwe!* His ears like twigs caught on small branches, stretching them. *Kwe!* His tail like a bush stuck to a large limb and pulled off. *Kwe!* His legs like sticks hit the ground and got shorter, much shorter in the front.

Now, our friend Gwa-io, the rabbit, looked like Rabbit!

Ever since that day, Rabbit's long ears bend with the wind; his legs, shorter in front than back, can hop; and his tail, like a ball of white fluff, is a small reminder of what he left behind.

Look closely at a willow tree in spring. Those tiny bits of gray fur, puffed out on slender shoots of the tall willow, come from the tail of Gwa-io, the rabbit who was tricked by Snow.

UNDER THE LOG
Winnebago

Once some mice lived under a log;
they had never been anywhere else, so they thought
that place was the world.
They thought that they were the only creatures in all
the world.
One of them stood on tiptoe; he stretched his little
arms up until he was able to touch the underside of
the log.

He thought he was very tall and that he had touched
the sky; so the little mouse danced and sang:
        "Throughout the world
        who is there like little me?
        Who is like me?
        I can touch the sky.
        I touch the sky, indeed."

THE GREAT PLAINS

Tall grasses, bending and rolling like gentle waves in the sea, covered the territory of the Great Plains, in the midsection of North America. This region reached from northern Alberta and Saskatchewan south to Texas. Where the tall grasses grew, the sky seemed endless, for there were no thick forests of tall trees to get in the way. But there *were* buffalo. A member of the Sioux Nation once said that there were so many that it took three whole days for a herd to go thundering by. The ground trembled and shook like an earthquake as they passed, and the noise was like a storm. This mighty beast provided food, clothing, shelter, and even fuel for all the native peoples who once lived in this part of the land. Their dependence on the buffalo for all their needs kept them from staying in one place too long. Their tipis could quickly be packed up and moved as they followed the herds.

High above the land soared many eagles, who were sacred to the tribes of the Plains. In the ceremonial song "The Gift of Peace," the eagle is shown to be their messenger to the Great Spirit. It is said that only Eagle can fly high enough to reach the home of Wakan Tanka, the Great Mystery, and so he must always be treated with deep respect.

FATHER IS COMING
Pawnee

Kawas! Your baby is crying!
Kawas! Your baby is crying!
Wailing and weeping,
your baby is crying!

Cry no more,
Father is coming!
Cry no more, Father is near.
The mighty one, Father, is coming.

TWO RACCOONS
Omaha

Two raccoons were walking along. The elder raccoon sang
a song:

> "Younger brother coon,
> let's go eat grapes,
> younger brother coon."

Younger brother coon said,

> "No, elder brother coon, I don't want to.
> My teeth chatter so whenever I eat them."

Then the elder raccoon sang:

> "Younger brother coon,
> let's go eat plums,
> younger brother coon."

Younger brother coon said,

> "No, elder coon, I don't want to.
> I get sick whenever I eat them."

Then the elder raccoon sang:

> "Younger brother coon,
> let's go eat chokeberries,
> younger brother coon."

Younger brother coon said,

"No, elder coon, I don't want to.
I get cold whenever I eat them."
Then the elder raccoon sang:
        "Younger brother coon,
        let's go eat crabs,
        younger brother coon."
Younger brother coon said,
        "Oh, elder brother coon! Oh, elder brother coon!
        Oh, elder brother coon! I like crabs!"
So off they went, down to the water, down to the water
where the crabs would come.
Then the elder raccoon said:
        "Play dead.
        If crabs tickle you, don't move.
        If crabs put their claws up your nose,
        don't move.
        Only move when I say 'Oho.'"
The two raccoons lay very very still.
Soon crabs came down to the water, down to the water
where they saw raccoons.
So they ran home and shouted,
        "Two raccoons lying dead over there,
        lying dead over there,
        hurrah!"

The whole village came down to the water, down to the water to see. One crab tickled the younger, tickled the younger, but he didn't move. Another stuck his claw in the

elder, stuck his claw in the elder, but he didn't move.
So the crabs began to dance, round and round, in a circle.
The whole village danced around the two raccoons.

"OHO!"
The raccoons jumped up.

They both jumped up and, *KRAKA KRAKA KRUNCH!*
They ate all but two!

TWO MICE
Sioux

Once there were two prairie mice. The first mouse was hardworking. During harvest each morning, she filled an empty cast-off snakeskin with ground beans, then dragged it home with her teeth.

The other mouse was lazy and careless. She danced around the campfires and talked all night long. By morning, she was too tired to gather beans. When an early frost reminded her that winter was coming, she ran to the other mouse for help.

The hardworking mouse asked, "Where were you during the moon when snakes cast off their skins? You have no bag to gather beans."

The lazy mouse answered, "I was here, but I was busy dancing and talking."

The hardworking mouse gave the lazy mouse a snakeskin and told her to waste no more time. The lazy mouse ran off to gather beans, but winter came so quickly that she went hungry.

Work before pleasure makes life better.

THE GIFT OF PEACE
Oto

Far above the earth he soars,
circling the clear sky,
flying over forests dim,
peering in shadows,
seeking far and wide his children,
to give them peace.

APPENDIX

A list of the tribes that appear in this book

It may be useful to understand certain terminology before reading the following descriptions. *Tribe* refers to a group of native peoples who share a common linguistic and cultural heritage. *League, nation,* and *confederacy* generally have the same meaning—a joining together of separate tribes who share the same political and social structure. However, many tribes are not members of any particular nation, and certain single tribes, such as the Dine (Navajo), call themselves nations rather than tribes.

Most of these tribes (or nations) were given names by those who first had contact with them. Names like Cherokee or Navajo were not what they actually called themselves. I have tried to include the original name of each tribe and, when at all possible, to explain its derivation. However, the origins of some are not known.

BEAVER (BEE-ver)

Although the name Beaver was given to this tribe by the Chippewa, they call themselves Deneza, which means "real people." They hunted beaver for furs and food, and moose or caribou when these could be found. Their winter lodges consisted of logs covered with moss and sod. After the Alaska Highway was built in 1942, most attended schools and learned English. Today quite a few earn a living by clearing brush for roads, pipelines, and power lines or acting as guides for big-game hunters in the Subarctic region of western Canada.

CHEROKEE (CHEHR-uh-kee)

They call themselves Aniyunwiyah, or "The Principal People." Some say the name Cherokee came from the Choctaw word meaning "cave dwellers." Originally, they lived in the Appalachian Mountains and in small villages along the rivers. Their conical houses were made of wood and mud. They wore turbans decorated with feathers, rather than the headbands worn by a number of other tribes.

The Indian Removal Act of 1830 drove the Cherokee westward so that white settlers could have their rich farmland. A third of them died in the long winter march known as the Trail of Tears. Some managed to hide or escape; their descendants now live on a large reservation in North Carolina.

CREEK

Early English traders gave them the name Creek because these native peoples built their villages on woodland rivers and creeks. In reality, the Creek were not just one group but consisted of different bands with many names. The Creek Confederacy, the largest in the Southeast, spread from Georgia to northern Alabama. Each band, such as the Taskigi (tass-KEE-gee), lived in farm towns, with their slanted-roof houses built around a square used for ceremonies, games, and festivities. Primarily farmers, they built granaries and warehouses beside their homes for storage.

In the Creek War, fought during the early 1800s, the Yuchi (YUH-kee) joined the Taskigi and other Creek led by Tecumseh to resist white domination. By 1840, they were removed to Indian Territory, which is now in eastern Oklahoma.

DINE (dih-NEE) "The People"

Popularly called Navajo (NAH-vuh-ho), a name given to them by the Spanish, they are believed to have moved from Canada to the Southwest during the 1300s. Today they are trying to establish Dine, which is what they have always called themselves, as their legal name. With a population of over 130,000, they are the largest tribe in the United States. Known the world over as weavers, potters, and silversmiths, many are also lawyers, surgeons, farmers, and teachers. Their reservation in Arizona is self-sufficient, with its own schools, hospitals, shops, and industries. The Dine are trying hard to retain their traditional ways, separate from the Western world. Since 1969, they have been officially called the Navajo Nation, with cultural and political autonomy not unlike that of each of the fifty states. They maintain an office in Washington devoted to the interests of all native peoples.

DUWAMISH (doo-WAHM-ish) "The River People"

This tiny tribe, who call themselves Dwamp'sh, once lived along rivers and the shores of what is now Lake Union in downtown Seattle. Fish was their primary food source, but they also hunted birds, deer, and elk. Usually they lived in plank houses with shedlike roofs. Having gained recognition as a tribe by the U.S. Bureau of Indian Affairs, the Duwamish continue to hold on to their traditional culture.

HAIDA (HI-duh) "The People"

The Haida, who live on the Queen Charlotte Islands, situated about ninety miles off the coast of British Columbia, are known as carvers of magnificent dugout canoes and totem poles. They originally lived in red cedar houses with elaborately carved corner posts and roof timbers. A totem pole up to fifty feet in height normally stood against the house facade.

Today many have had to leave the islands in order to find employment in the large cities of British Columbia. Of those who remain on the islands, many work in the fishing or lumber industries. The older members are doing their best to teach younger generations their ancient customs and traditions, but the amenities of our modern civilization are tempting and sometimes get in the way.

INUIT (IN-yoo-it) "The People"

Known to the rest of the world as Eskimo, these peoples inhabit Greenland, northern Canada, the Subarctic, Alaska, and parts of Siberia. Great hunters of seal and caribou, they once traveled by kayak or dogsled, but now use snowmobiles to skim across the frozen earth. Some still build igloos when they go hunting, but most live in houses with heat and electricity, and many now reside in Anchorage, Alaska.

The Aleut (AL-ee-oot), a branch of the Inuit, live on the chain of islands between Siberia and Alaska. The Russians gave them the name Aleut, which means "island," but they call themselves Unangan, or "Those of the Seaside." They once lived in large log houses, divided into family "apartments" with a common room in the center and built partially underground for warmth. They bathed in the cold water of streams nearby and wore shoes only during the bitterest days of winter.

LENAPE (leh-NAW-pee) "The Ordinary People"

Also known as the Delaware, the Lenape once occupied what is now New York City, New Jersey, eastern Pennsylvania, and Delaware, where fish and game were abundant and the seasons neither too long nor too short. These deeply religious people lived in small family groupings and led a tranquil existence, avoiding conflict whenever possible; they were immensely kind to the early settlers. Like other Woodlands tribes, the Lenape lived in long houses, particularly during the winter months. In the summer, they camped by the shore, where they caught lobsters and clams. Today an estimated 2,000 Lenape still live in New Jersey, Pennsylvania, and Delaware, but most had migrated to the Midwest by 1737, when whites claimed their land, eventually settling on reservations in Kansas and Oklahoma.

NEZ PERCE (nehz purse) "Pierced Nose"

The Nez Perce (so called by the French because many of them wore nose pendants) lived in the mountains of Washington, Oregon, and Idaho. Their name for themselves is Nimipu, which means "the people." Originally, they were hunters and gatherers who moved their village sites with the changing seasons. They did not make pottery, but wove exquisite baskets, which they used for cooking by placing heated stones in them.

In the early 1700s, when they acquired horses through trade, the Nez Perce became skilled horse trainers and breeders. Guided by their famous Chief Joseph, they tried valiantly to live peacefully with the white settlers, but their highly valued land, full of gold and ore, was seized. Their chief pleaded to let his people stay, but the whites wanted no part of this. "The only good Indian is a dead Indian" became a national slogan. After many Nez Perce were massacred, the survivors, starving and exhausted, were forced to walk to a distant reservation in Idaho, where their descendants now live.

OJIBWA (oh-JIB-way)

Ojibwa was an English rendering of a word that meant "puckered up," used to describe the moccasins this tribe wore. Originally calling themselves Anishinabe, or "The People," they are known as the Ojibwa in Canada and the Chippewa (CHIP-uh-wah) in the United States. With a population of over 160,000, the Ojibwa are one of the largest groups of native people in North America today. Although many have moved to urban areas, a large number remain on several reservations. There is still a strong connection between them, and great emphasis is placed upon teaching the children about their heritage. Their dome-shaped, bark-covered wigwams were once a familiar sight in the northern Great Lakes area, where they traveled to hunt or barter. Since wood was so accessible, most of their craftwork was made out of birch bark, including their canoes. Today wild rice and maple sugar are among their commercial enterprises.

OMAHA (OH-muh-haw) "Those Going Against the Current"

This Plains tribe originally lived in the Ohio Valley and the prairie lands along the northern Mississippi and its tributaries. But the Eastern Woodlands tribes, driven westward by the settlers, fought the Omaha and other tribes in this region and took their land. So the Omaha moved farther west and settled along the Missouri River. Here they farmed and built villages of earth lodges grouped together. They also fished, and sometimes left their villages to search for buffalo. In 1854, the Omaha ceded all their lands west of the Missouri River to the United States and were settled on a reservation in Nebraska. There are about 1,500 still living there today.

OTO (OH-toe) "Lecher"

Originally the Oto, who were members of the Great Sioux Confederacy, were one people with the Winnebago, Iowa, and Missouri. When this large group pushed westward, they divided into separate tribes. This final split supposedly occurred when two chiefs quarreled because the son of one ran off with the daughter of another. This is how the Oto got their name.

Like other Plains people, they stayed in one spot during the winter months, living in earth houses built partially underground for warmth. Smoke holes enabled them to cook indoors. They hunted buffalo, their main life support, following the herds and living in tipis, which could easily be set up and taken down. Today most of them are on reservations in Oklahoma.

PAWNEE (paw-NEE) "Horn"

The Pawnee were a federation of tribes who inhabited river valleys of Nebraska and Kansas until the nineteenth century. They planted corn and hunted buffalo. They were given their name by other tribes because they wore their hair in a stiff hornlike coil, shaped with grease. They call themselves Chahiksichohiks, which means "men of men." Once numbering over 25,000, they lost half their population when settlers arrived bringing diseases like cholera with them. Even though many Pawnee served as scouts for the U.S. Army during the Plains Indian Wars, their people were forced to settle on reservations in Oklahoma, where just over 1,000 of them still live.

PUEBLO (PWEHB-lo) "Village"

Pueblo is the Spanish name for the various tribes who live in adobe dwellings grouped together and shaped roughly like tall apartment complexes. The six Pueblo villages that belong to the Tewa (TAY-wuh) are located near the Rio Grande. Primarily farmers, they raise corn, squash, beans, and other crops, but they are known throughout the world for their exquisite pottery, woven rugs, and baskets. Their way of life remains deeply religious and traditional.

The Tigua (TEE-wah) are Pueblo peoples who left their homeland in New Mexico when whites arrived during the mid-1800s, migrating to western Texas and finally to Arizona, where they have their own reservation today. They remain traditional, still performing centuries-old ceremonies and religious rites. Like all Pueblo cultures, they continue to weave fine baskets and make their own pottery.

SENECA (SEN-ih-kuh) "Place of the Stone"

The Seneca once lived in long houses around Lake Erie and along the Allegheny River. They called themselves Onotwa'ka, or "People of the Big Hill." Their women were always treated with respect, as equals to men, and still hold powerful decision-making positions. They were the largest member tribe of the Iroquois League of Six Nations, whose constitution influenced the formation of American democracy and the U.S. Constitution. The symbol for the Iroquois League was a "tree of peace," a giant white pine drawn with an eagle on top holding five arrows, which appears on the U.S. quarter. The Seneca have several reservations in northern New York State.

SHASTA (SHAS-tuh)

This group of small peaceful tribes lived in the valley of Mount Shasta in what is now Northern California and along the Klamath River in southern Oregon. Their permanent villages consisted of houses dug partially underground, then covered with wooden plank sidings and roofs. They foraged for roots, acorns, seeds, and berries, and fished for salmon. Sometimes they ate crickets and grasshoppers, and used milkweed as a chewing gum. The women, who wore woven hats and three stripes tattooed on their chins, were also their doctors. Their storytelling was primarily to entertain children, and the teller of tales was usually a grandmother. During the mid-1800s, the gold miners, greedy for the Shasta's land, virtually wiped them out.

SIOUX (soo) "Snake"

The name the Sioux call themselves is Ocheti Shakowin, or "The Seven Council Fires." The Great Sioux Nation consists of three main divisions: the Dakota, Nakota, and Lakota. Within each of these are numerous tribes, individually named, such as the Oglala, who are Lakota. The Sioux lived mostly in tipis and, like the buffalo they hunted, moved constantly. When the whites who wished to settle and farm this fertile land arrived, the Sioux wanted a peaceful coexistence. Chiefs like Red Cloud, Sitting Bull, and Crazy Horse tried to negotiate settlements, but each time they were betrayed. In the battles that followed, many lives were lost. It was the Lakota who fought fiercely, despite great odds, and finally defeated General Custer at Little Bighorn in 1876. Meanwhile, hunters hired by the U.S. government sought to exterminate the buffalo so as to starve the native peoples and force them into submission. Then, at Wounded Knee in 1890, the U.S. military massacred the Sioux, many of whom were unarmed. This tragic event marked the end of the wars between the native peoples and the U.S. government, forcing those who remained to live on reservations.

Despite all this, the Sioux Nation has grown and strengthened over the years. There are 40,000 living on reservations in Oklahoma and South Dakota; their leaders are involved in litigation to regain land taken from them illegally—particularly the Black Hills of South Dakota, which they consider sacred. They are also trying to reestablish buffalo herds in parts of the Great Plains.

SLAVEY (SLAY-vee) "Slave"

Their name was derived from the Cree word for "captive." The Slavey once lived in low, oblong cabins made of logs, with pitched roofs covered with spruce. Gathering in small groups of ten or twenty, they built their homes near ponds, where they fished. In the summer, they would all get together and camp on the shores of Great Slave Lake. Related linguistically to the Plains tribes located farther south, they still live deep inside the wilderness of western Canada. In the late seventies, the Slavey became active in local politics when plans were made for the Mackenzie pipeline to go through their land. As a result of their involved opposition, the construction of the pipeline was halted. Their harsh, cold region, considered uninhabitable by most, is not good for farming, so the 3,000 or so who remain there today spend much of their time hunting, fishing, and trapping.

TLINGIT (KLING-kit) "The People"

The Tlingit still live along the coast of the Alaska panhandle and retain many of the rich traditions of their past. They are great carvers, particularly of totem poles, and creators of fine baskets and Chilkat button blankets. The blankets are woven out of cedar bark and mountain-goat hair. Most of their food comes from the sea. Their houses, made of wooden logs, are sometimes large enough to hold several hundred people.

WINNEBAGO (win-uh-BAY-go) "People Near the Dirty Water"

Although the Winnebago are Siouan-speaking, they are actually related to the Eastern Woodlands tribes. In the early 1800s, they migrated to the eastern part of what is now Wisconsin, where they farmed and hunted buffalo. The Winnebago were friendly with the British and French and helped fight their battles, such as the War of Independence. Nevertheless, they were forced to live separately from the whites, and after being moved six times, they were finally settled on a reservation in Nebraska, where today fewer than 1,000 remain.

WISHOSK (WEESH-ahsk)

The Wishosk, who lived along the shores of Humboldt Bay where Eureka, California, is now located, were given this name by the first explorers. Then, in 1854, ethnologists renamed them Wiyot, even though they called themselves Sulatlek. The meanings of all these names are unknown. The Wishosk lived on quiet waters, like ponds or bays, and depended on fish and small game for sustenance. Their clothing was usually made from buckskin, similar to that worn by Eastern Woodlands tribes. Sometimes they adorned themselves with intricately twined, dome-shaped basketry hats. Two or more families usually occupied a rectangular dwelling made from split redwood planks. Overrun by gold miners, these people were rapidly killed off during the mid-1800s.

SOURCE NOTES

"A Story!"
This was collected by Franz Boas in the Cumberland Sound in 1883 and published in the *Journal of American Folklore,* Volume 10, 1897, under the title "Eskimo Tales and Songs."

"Fox Fools Eagle," "Land in the Sky," and "Why Fox Is Red"
These were part of a collection in a book called *Myths and Legends of Alaska,* written by Katharine Berry Judson and published in 1911 by A. C. McClurg. "Land in the Sky" is my rendering of the legend called "The Chief in the Moon," which originated somewhere in the Bering Straits. "Fox Fools Eagle" was first told by the Koryak in Siberia. "Why Fox Is Red" was also published under the title "Athapascan Traditions" by Houghton Mifflin, for the American Folklore Society, in 1901, published in the *Journal of American Folklore,* Volume 16.

"Firefly Song"
This was translated by Henry Schoolcraft in his book *Myth of Hiawatha,* published by J. B. Lippincott, Philadelphia, in 1856, and in his collection of Ojibwa songs.

"The Long Winter"
This tale was collected by Robert Bell and published in the *Journal of American Folklore,* Volume 14, 1901, under the title "Legends of the Slavey Indians of the Mackenzie River." My retelling includes dialogue between the animals that was based on the original narrative.

"The Wind Song"
My adaptation is actually a combination of the wind song, rain song, and song of the pines that were in W. S. Philips's book *Indian Fairy Tales,* published by the Star Publishing Company, Chicago, 1902.

"Raven, the River Maker" and "No Frogs At All"
These come from "Tales from the Totems of the Hidery," collected by James Deans and published in the *Archives of the International Folklore Association,* Volume 2, Chicago, 1899. My adaptation of "No Frogs At All" includes additional dialogue that was not in the narrative of the original translation.

"How Beaver Stole Fire"
This legend was told to R. L. Packard in 1880 at the Ponca Agency by James Reubens, a Nez Perce, who was also interpreter for Chief Joseph's band. This was subsequently published under the title "Mythology and Religion of the Nez Perces" in the *Journal of American Folklore,* Volume 4, 1891.

"Why Frogs Swim"
This was first told to me by my grandfather, but a similar version is in *The North American Indian,* Volume 13, Cambridge University Press, 1924.

"How Spider Caught Flies"
An old man named Bill related this tale to A. L. Kroeber at the turn of the century. It is part of a collection entitled "Wishosk Myths" published in 1905 in the *Journal of American Folklore,* Volume 18. Originally called "Gudatrigakwitl (Who Was the Creator) and the Spider," the translation was a brief paragraph, which I expanded by adding dialogue.

"The Corn Song"

This is a condensed version of verses sung between the narration of a myth of the Garden of the House God. It was translated and collected by Washington Mathews in 1894 for the *Journal of American Folklore,* Volume 7.

"Coyote and the Blackbirds"

There are numerous sources for this story, but I used the version told to Charles Lummis in his book *Pueblo Indian Folk Stories,* which was published by the Century Company, New York, in 1910. I added dialogue and sound effects to enhance the suspense in this humorous tale.

"The Mockingbird Song"

This was translated by Alice Fletcher, a noted ethnologist, in her book *Indian Story and Song from North America,* published by Small, Maynard, Boston, 1900. It was sung by a Tigua girl of the pueblo of Isleta, New Mexico.

"Mother Sun"

This was recorded by John R. Swanton in his "Myths and Tales of the Southeastern Indians" in the *Bulletin of the Bureau of American Ethnology,* Number 88, 1929. It is a creation legend, sparsely told, which I rewrote in poetic form.

"A Tug of War"

Recorded by Frank G. Speck in his collection entitled "The Creek Indians of Taskigi Town," this was published in the *American Anthropological Society Memoirs,* 2:2, in 1907. Like Coyote and Raven, Rabbit is the trickster of the Southeast. A tie snake is some sort of water moccasin, very wide in body and immensely strong. Mentioned in numerous legends of the Southeast, it may be a variant of their mythological horned water serpent. This tale seems to have originated in Africa, for it mentions getting water from wells, a common source of conflict in the stories told there. It is much like one told in the Congo about Tortoise, who pits Elephant against Hippopotamus.

"How Possum Got His Skinny Tail"

This was recorded by James Mooney in the *Bulletin of the Bureau of American Ethnology,* Number 21, in 1900. I was also told a similar version of this story by a storyteller from Lumbee, North Carolina.

"The Earth on Turtle's Back," "Rabbit and the Willow," and "Under the Log"

These were told to me by various storytellers in the Northeast, including Bill Whip-poor-will Thompson, a Lenape elder. Jesse Cornplanter told a similar version of "Rabbit and the Willow" in his book *Longhouse Tales.*

"Father Is Coming"

The Pawnee sang this during a special ceremony created for "a crying child who could not be comforted." The *kawas,* a fan of eagle feathers, was placed on a cougar skin as the song was sung. (The eagle was their messenger to the Great Spirit.) The father in this song is the Great Spirit, who is being asked to quiet the child. It was said that any child who heard this song immediately stopped crying and was comforted. Translated by Alice Fletcher, this was published in her book *Indian Story and Song from North America* in 1900.

"Two Raccoons"

The earliest complete translation of this song/tale can be found in "The Cegiha Language": U.S. Geographical and Geological Survey of the Rocky Mountain Region, *Contributions to North American Ethnology,* Volume 6,

Washington GPO, recorded in 1890 by James Owen Dorsey. He also published a shorter version in the *Journal of American Folklore,* Volume 2, 1889. A Seneca version, in the form of a play called *Coon Deceives Crawfish,* was done by Jeremiah Curtin in his book *Seneca Indian Myths,* published by E. P. Dutton, New York, 1923. Since there are numerous tellings by different tribes, there is no way to prove that the Omaha version used here is the first translation, but it was transcribed earlier than others I found.

"Two Mice"

This fable was told by Marie L. McLaughlin, who was of Sioux ancestry, in her book *Myths and Legends of the Sioux,* published by the Bismarck Tribune Company, North Dakota, in 1916.

"The Gift of Peace"

This song was part of a sacred ceremony performed by the Oto. It was sung when the calumets, which were shaped like pipes and considered holy, were laid to rest on wildcat skins. This song accompanied the movements of the calumets. The calumet was a powerful symbol for peace. If one was held up between two warring tribes, everyone immediately dropped their weapons. This song was collected by ethnologist Alice Fletcher in *Indian Story and Song from North America.*

ADDITIONAL REFERENCES

Burland, Cottie. *Mythology of the Americas,* Hamlyn Publishing Group, London, 1970.

Catlin, George. *North American Indians,* reprint of 1844 edition, Dover Publications, 1973.

Cronyn, George W. *American Indian Poetry,* Ballantine Books, reprint of 1918 edition, 1991.

Curtis, Edward S. *The North American Indian,* The University Press, Cambridge, Mass., 1924.

Damas, David. *Arctic Handbook of North American Indians,* Volume 5, Smithsonian Institution, 1985.

Dutton, Bertha P. *American Indians of the Southwest,* University of Mexico Press, 1983.

Erdoes, Richard. *American Indian Myths and Legends,* Pantheon, 1984.

Gattuso, John. *Native America,* Houghton Mifflin, 1993.

Haines, Francis. *The Buffalo,* Thomas Y. Crowell Company, 1970.

King, Duane. *The Cherokee Indian Nation: A Troubled History,* University of Tennessee Press, 1979.

Kopper, Philip. *The Smithsonian Book of North American Indians,* Smithsonian Institution, 1986.

Lindig, Wolfgang. *Navajo: Tradition and Change in the Southwest,* Facts on File (translated from the German, 1993).

Marriot, Alice. *American Indian Mythology,* New American Library, 1972.

Maxwell, James A. *America's Fascinating Indian Heritage,* Reader's Digest Association, 1978.

Parker, Arthur. *Seneca Myths and Folktales,* University of Nebraska Press, 1989.

Renfro, Elizabeth. *The Shasta Indians of California and Their Neighbors,* Naturegraph Publishers, 1992.

Spence, Lewis. *The Myths of the North American Indian,* reprint of 1914 edition, Dover Publications, 1989.

Spicer, Edward H. *The American Indians,* Harvard University Press, 1982.

Sturtevant, William C. *Handbook of North American Indians,* Smithsonian Institution, 1978–90.

Thomas, David Hurst. *The Native Americans: An Illustrated History,* Turner Publishing, 1993.

Turner, Frederick. *The Portable North American Indian Reader,* Viking Press, 1977.

Weslager, C. A. *The Delaware Indians,* Rutgers University Press, 1990.